Reading Bridge™

2nd grade

Written by

Meadow Bond

Reading Bridge™
2nd Grade

Please visit our website at
www.summerbridgeactivities.com
for supplements, additions, and corrections to this book.

Series Creator
Michele D. Van Leeuwen

Cover Inset Art
Joe Flores

Production and Layout
Andy Carlson, Robyn Funk, Amanda Sorensen

Copy Editors/Proofreaders
Kathleen Bratcher, Kim Carlson, Dorothy Duckworth, Suzie Ellison,
Ben Fulton, Paul Rawlins, Debby Reed

Special Thanks
Dante J. Orazzi

The author would like to gratefully acknowledge the assistance & suggestions of the following:
Carla Dawn Fisher, Dr. Leland Graham, Julia Ann Hobbs

Printed in the United States of America

ISBN 1-887923-51-9

10 9 8 7 6 5 4 3

Table of Contents

Introduction

The **Reading Bridge**™ series is designed to improve and motivate student reading. This book has been developed to provide second grade students practical, skill-based exercises in the areas of inferences, main ideas, cause and effect, fact and opinion, and figurative language and to familiarize students with the kinds of reading tasks they will encounter on a daily basis. Furthermore, reading will enrich and facilitate their lives as young adults in an ever-changing world that has information readily available, but only if they learn to take advantage of and appreciate reading.

The stories, poems, essays, and puzzles in this collection are accompanied by exercises that help students develop reading skills. The carefully thought-out questions will help your students learn to think, inquire, create, imagine, respond, and, in some instances, do research to learn more about a specific topic.

Reading Bridge™ adapts to any teaching situation whether at home or in the classroom. It can be used in many different ways:

- ✔ **For at-home practice:** this series is ideal for supplementing or expanding upon schoolwork and home-school reading programs.

- ✔ **For the entire class:** this series can be used for intensive reinforcement of reading skills or to supplement a Basal Reading Program.

- ✔ **For reading groups:** this series will provide skills practice at appropriate levels, and the reading exercises become progressively more challenging.

- ✔ **For individual use:** this series can help you build a completely individualized program.

Use Your Dictionary!

The English language is made up of thousands and thousands of words, so many words that it would be impossible for you to know what every single one of these words means! But wait! Just because you come across a word in this book, or somewhere else, that may be unfamiliar to you does not mean that you should ignore it or give up on learning its meaning.

Instead, use a dictionary to learn the meaning of the word you don't know. You'll get better scores on the exercises in this book. More importantly, you'll expand your knowledge base and become a better communicator because you'll be able to both express yourself and understand other people more clearly!

Dic • tio • nary, n. 1. a book of alphabetically listed words in a language, with definitions, pronunciation, and other information about the words.

2nd Grade Reading List

Adler, David
Cam Jansen and the Mystery of the Dinosaur Bones

Aliki
Mummies Made in Egypt

Allard, Harry
Miss Nelson books

Andersen, Hans Christian
The Emperor's New Clothes

Barrett, Judi
Cloudy with a Chance of Meatballs

Barracca, Debra
The Adventures of Taxi Dog

Berenstain, Stan & Jan
The Berenstain Bears books

Bond, Michael
Paddington Bear series

Byars, Betsy Cromer
Hooray for the Golly Sisters!
The Golly Sisters Go West
My Brother, Ant
The chapter books

Caudill, Rebecca
A Pocket full of Cricket

Coerr, Eleanor
Chang's Paper Pony

Cole, Joanna
Big Goof and Little Goof

Crummel, Susan Stevens
Tumbleweed Stew

Cushman, Doug
Aunt Eater's Mystery Vacation

Delton, Judy
Pee Wee Scout books

Dooley, Norah
Everybody Cooks Rice

Flack, Marjorie
The Story about Ping

Fraustino, Lisa Rowe
The Hickory Chair

The Funny Side Up books
Dinosaur Jokes
Knock, Knock Jokes
School Jokes
Space Jokes
Sports Jokes

Holabird, Katherine
Angelina Ballerina

Jonas, Ann
Aardvarks, Disembark

Gackenbach, Dick
Mag the Magnificent

Griffith, Helen V.
Alex and the Cat

Hoban, Lillian
Arthur books

Hoff, Syd
The Horse in Harry's Room

Hutchins, Pat
Don't Forget the Bacon

Kimmel, Eric A.
The Chanukkah Guest

Keats, Ezra Jack
John Henry, American Legend
Maggie and the Pirate

2nd Grade Reading List

Komakio, Leah
Annie Bananie

Kuskin, Karla
Soap Soup

Lobel, Arnold
The Frog and Toad series
Ming Lo Moves the Mountain

Leaf, Munro
The Story of Ferdinand

McCully, Emily Arnold
Zaza's Big Break

Mayer, Mercer
Just Me books

Miles, Miska
Annie and the Old One

Mozelle, Shirley
Zack's Alligator

O'Connor, Jane
Super Cluck
Teeny Tiny Woman

Parish, Peggy
Amelia Bedelia books

Pickett, Anola
Old Enough for Magic

Platt, Kin
Big Max

Rathmann, Peggy
Officer Buckle and Gloria

Rey, H. A.
The Curious George series

Roop, Peter and Connie
Keep the Lights Burning, Abbie

Sachar, Louis
Marvin Redpost books

Schwartz, Alvin
Busy Buzzing Bumblebees and Other
    Tongue Twisters
There Is a Carrot in My Ear and Other
    Noodle Tales
In a Dark, Dark Room and Other Scary
    Stories
All of Our Noses are Here and Other
    Noodle Stories
I Saw You in the Bathtub and Other
    Folk Rhymes

Sharmat, Mitchell
Gregory, the Terrible Eater

Sharmat, Majorie Weinman
A Big, Fat Enormous Lie

Small, David
Imogene's Antlers

Steig, William
The Zabajaba Jungle

Titus, Eve
Anatole books

Turner, Ann Warren
Dust for Dinner

Waber, Bernard
Bernard

Williams, Margery
The Velveteen Rabbit

Zion, Gene
Harry by the Sea

Incentive Contract

In • 'cen • tive, n. **1.** Something that urges a person on. **2.** Enticing. **3.** Encouraging. **4.** That which excites to action or moves the mind.

Below, list your agreed-upon incentive for each section.
Place a ✔ after each exercise upon completion.

Page	Activity Title	✔
8	Eli	
10	Arden's Surprise	
13	Twins	
15	The Zoo	
18	Pillow Fight	
20	Bats	
22	The Summer Plan	
25	The Lonely Turtle	

My Incentive Is:

Page	Story & Exercise Title	✔
49	The Koala	
51	Costume Party	
53	Rudy Gets Lost	
56	Teddy	
58	Germs	
61	Ed and Emily	
64	Nana's Gift	
67	Lucas	

My Incentive Is:

Page	Story & Exercise Title	✔
28	Two	
30	Marvin the Moose	
33	Lizzy's Song	
37	Nikki the Dog	
40	Lemonade	
43	The Rain	
45	Insects	
47	The Pumpkin Patch	

My Incentive Is:

Page	Story & Exercise Title	✔
70	Who's There?	
72	Amazing Ants	
74	Sea Dreams	
77	Americans in History	
80	A Little Brother	
83	Olivia's Dance	
87	Cameron Crow	
91	The Gift	

My Incentive Is:

Student Signature

Teacher, Parent or Guardian Signature

_____

_____

ELI

Eli is a big dog. His coat is tan, white, and brown. Usually, when you see Eli, his tongue will be hanging out. This is because he is always playing. He likes to chase the ball, and he likes to roll around, but most of all, Eli likes to go to the river.

Every Saturday morning, Eli's owner, Julianne, takes him to the park by the river to play. Eli rides in the back of the car with his head out the window. His tongue hangs out of his mouth and flaps in the wind. The first thing Eli does when they get to the river is run down to the water. Eli likes to take a drink and splash around. Next he will usually chase some of the other dogs that have come to play. After he has played and played, Eli will take a nap under the picnic table while Julianne and her friends enjoy a picnic.

On the way home, Eli does not hang his head out of the window. Instead, he lies down on the backseat. He sleeps the whole way home, dreaming of the excitement he will have next Saturday.

Reading Challenge

After reading "Eli," answer the following questions.

1. **Which of the following is not something the story told us Eli likes to do?**
   - ○ A. chase the ball
   - ○ B. bury bones
   - ○ C. go to the river
   - ○ D. roll around

2. **Which of the following best describes Eli?**
   - ○ A. a tan, white, and brown dog that is mean
   - ○ B. a small dog that likes to swim
   - ○ C. a lazy dog who barks a lot
   - ○ D. a big and playful dog

3. **Place a 1, 2, 3, or 4 on the line beside each sentence to put the events in the correct order.**

   _____ Eli takes a nap under the picnic table.

   _____ Eli runs down to the water.

   _____ Eli hangs his head out of the window.

   _____ Eli chases some of the other dogs.

4. **The story tells us that Eli does not hang his head out of the window on the way home. Why do you think this is?**

   _____

5. **Draw and color a picture of Eli in the space below.**

Total Correct _____

Arden's Surprise

Today was Mom's birthday, and Arden wanted to surprise her. She made her a card, but she wanted to do something more, something special. Arden thought and thought about what to do. Suddenly, it came to her. She would make Mom a treat to eat!

The family rules were that no cooking was allowed when there wasn't an adult in the kitchen. Arden couldn't ask for Mom's help. That would ruin the surprise, so she had to make a treat that she wouldn't have to cook.

First Arden looked in the refrigerator. There was some milk, some orange juice, a little bit of cheese, and some strawberries. Arden pulled all of these things out and put them on the counter. Next, she looked in the pantry. There she found some cereal, some cookies, a box of crackers, and some peanut butter.

Arden took out the mixing bowl. She poured in a little milk, a little orange juice, and added a big spoonful of peanut butter. She stirred her mixture. When everything was mixed well, Arden added a few strawberries, some cheese, and a big handful of cereal. Last, she took out two cookies and spread the mixture between them. She exclaimed, "It's a cookie sandwich!"

Arden made three more cookie sandwiches: one for Dad, one for herself, and one for her baby sister, Cate. Just as Arden finished making the last cookie sandwich, Mom and Cate walked into the kitchen. Arden took her a cookie sandwich and sang "Happy Birthday." Mom was so surprised that she shouted, "Let's try one now!" Arden, Mom, and Cate sat at the table to eat their treats!

Mom tasted her cookie sandwich first. "Mmmm. This is very unusual, Arden. Tell me what you put in it," Mom said. Arden named all of the ingredients; then she tried a bite of her cookie sandwich. "Yuck!" said Arden. "This is nasty, Mom." Arden was just about to get upset when she noticed baby Cate reaching for another cookie. "Cate likes it," Mom said. Mom and Arden laughed and laughed as they watched Cate eat their cookie sandwiches.

Reading Challenge

After reading "Arden's Surprise," answer the following questions.

1. Why did Arden want to surprise Mom? _____

   _____

2. Why couldn't Arden ask Mom for help?

   _____

3. Draw a line under the items Arden used to make the cookie sandwiches.

   milk   cheese   marshmallows   strawberries

   orange juice   peanut butter   crackers   cereal

4. Why was Mom surprised?

   _____

5. What made Arden and Mom laugh?

   _____

6. Do you think Arden's dad will like the cookie sandwich? Why or why not?

   _____

   _____

Mix is the root or base word of mixing.
Write the root or base word for each word below.

7. swimming _____

8. baked _____

Total Correct _____

Twins

Twins

Chris and Will are twins. They are brothers who were born on the same day. Twins that look almost exactly alike are called identical twins. Chris and Will do look a little bit alike, but they are not identical twins. Chris and Will are fraternal twins, which means they were born on the same day but do not look exactly alike.

Will has curly red hair. Chris's hair is brown and straight. Chris has green eyes, and Will's eyes are blue. Another difference between them is their teeth. Chris is missing his two front teeth. Will has all of his teeth, and he has braces!

Both boys like to play baseball. Sometimes they play third base. Sometimes they play catcher. Both of them can throw the ball well. It can be fun to have a twin.

Reading Challenge

After reading "Twins," answer the following questions.

Read each phrase. If it describes Chris, write a <u>C</u> on the line. If it describes Will, write a <u>W</u> on the line. If the phrase describes both boys, write a <u>B</u> on the line.

1. _____ is a twin

2. _____ has red hair

3. _____ plays catcher

4. _____ missing two front teeth

5. _____ has green eyes

6. Draw a picture of each boy.

Chris

Will

7. What do you call twins that do not look exactly alike?

_____

8. Circle the words below that have a long vowel sound.

twin	red	base
teeth	play	fun
braces	Will	both

Total Correct _____

The Zoo

Every other Saturday, Martha's mother volunteers at the zoo. Martha loves going to the zoo with her mom. While her mother hands out maps to visitors, Martha gets to walk around and visit her animal friends.

Martha's first stop is the flamingos. She loves to watch them stand on one foot. The bird keeper told Martha that flamingos get their beautiful pink color from eating shrimp and other shellfish.

After watching the flamingos, Martha likes to visit the African Safari Exhibit. She likes to watch the graceful giraffe nibble leaves from the tops of the trees. Martha was scared the first time she saw the zebra chasing the gazelle, but soon she realized that they were only playing.

The gorilla are the most fun to watch. Some of the gorilla babies make faces at Martha if she stands still long enough. Two of the babies like to roll down the hill. Martha wishes that she could go into the gorilla habitat to roll down the hill with them.

The reptile house is next. Martha waits for her mom to finish volunteering before she goes inside. She knows that the reptiles won't hurt her, but she is still afraid to go in alone. When Mom is holding her hand, Martha likes to look at the snakes.

The Zoo, continued

The zoo has a carousel. Martha likes to ride around and around on it. This carousel is special. Instead of just horses, this carousel has different zoo animals you can ride. Martha always picks the gorilla.

On the ride home, Martha talks about how much fun she had at the zoo. When she grows up, she wants to be a veterinarian and help take care of animals. Until then, she will look forward to her next trip to the zoo!

Reading Challenge

After reading "The Zoo," answer the following questions.

1. **How often does Martha get to go to the zoo?**
   - ○ A. every other week
   - ○ B. once a month
   - ○ C. every Saturday
   - ○ D. once a year

2. **What does Martha's mom do while Martha visits the zoo?**
   - ○ A. She waits in the car.
   - ○ B. She walks around with Martha.
   - ○ C. She hands out zoo maps.
   - ○ D. She runs errands.

3. **Where does Martha go first?**
   - ○ A. the reptile house
   - ○ B. the flamingos
   - ○ C. the African Safari Exhibit
   - ○ D. the gorilla

4. **Which animals are Martha's favorite to watch?**
   - ○ A. the snakes
   - ○ B. the zebras
   - ○ C. the flamingos
   - ○ D. the gorilla

5. **How do flamingos get their pink color?**
   - ○ A. The zoo paints them.
   - ○ B. They swim in salt water.
   - ○ C. They eat shrimp and other shellfish.
   - ○ D. They are born that way.

6. **Why does Martha want to be a veterinarian when she grows up?**
   - ○ A. to make lots of money
   - ○ B. so she can go to the zoo by herself
   - ○ C. so she won't have to do her homework
   - ○ D. so she can be around animals

Total Correct _____

Pillow Fight

It's Friday night. School is out.
"Sleepover at my house!"
I hear myself shout.
My friends all yell, sing, and cheer
because we all know the weekend is here.

Outside we play until the sun goes down.
Hide-and-seek is fun.
We all clown around.
"It's late," Dad calls.
"You must come inside."
I was sad at first.
It was my turn to hide.

We eat pizza for dinner
and drink soda, too,
play board games, sing songs,
and learn something new.
Dad teaches a game that he used to play.
You can act and gesture,
but words you can't say.

It was my turn at last. I had an idea,
maybe the best one that I'd had in a year.
I picked up my pillow, held it over my head,
then I threw it at Dad.
"Look out!" someone yelled.

Before I knew it, we were all involved.
My word to act out
had just now been solved.
We playfully tossed our pillows
at each other,
popping a friend, then running for cover.

The place was a mess,
feathers all through the room.
Mom stood at the door, in her hand was a broom.
"Enough is enough," she said with a smile.
And we all helped to sweep
the mess in one pile.

Reading Challenge

After reading "Pillow Fight," answer the following questions.

1. Words that have the same middle and ending sounds are called rhyming words. <u>Bed</u> rhymes with <u>head</u>, and <u>bee</u> rhymes with <u>see</u>. Find at least three pairs of words that rhyme in the poem and write them on the lines below.

_____

_____

_____

2. What is the poem mostly about?
   - ○ A. eating pizza
   - ○ B. cleaning up the mess
   - ○ C. a sleepover party
   - ○ D. playing outside

3. Which of the following did not happen in the poem?
   - ○ A. There was a pillow fight.
   - ○ B. They told scary stories.
   - ○ C. They played hide-and-seek.
   - ○ D. They had pizza and soda for dinner.

4. Why is everyone excited at the beginning of the poem?

   _____

5. What would you like to do at a sleepover party?

   _____

   _____

   _____

   _____

Total Correct _____

BATS

Many people are afraid of things they do not know much about. That is why so many people are afraid of bats. People who have learned about bats are not afraid of them. They realize that bats are not harmful. They are, in fact, helpful.

Did you know that some bats eat insects? That's right. Bats help control the insect population by eating mosquitoes, gnats, and other pests. Not all bats eat insects. Some bats eat fruit. They are called fruit bats.

Bats are nocturnal. This means that they are active at night. Bats use echolocation to help get around. Echolocation happens when a bat makes a high-pitched sound. The sound bounces, or echoes, off objects. This helps the bat know how close or far away an object is.

There are many myths about bats. A myth is something that many people believe to be true, but may not be true at all. One myth is that if you go too close to a bat it will fly into your hair and get stuck! Bats are afraid of people. The last thing a bat wants is to be in your hair! Another myth is that bats bite people and suck their blood. There is a certain kind of bat, called a vampire bat, that lives on the blood of cows and other large animals; however, they rarely bite humans. These bats live in South America. Most bats don't like the taste of blood and stick to fruit or insects.

Even though bats are our friends, it is not a good idea to try to pet or catch a bat. Even the most helpful animals will bite if they are scared. Some animals carry diseases, and they can give the disease to humans if they bite. If you see a bat, it is okay to look, but don't touch, and remember, bats help us in many ways!

Reading Challenge

After reading "Bats," answer the following questions.

1. **Why are many people afraid of bats?**
   - ○ A. They don't know much about them.
   - ○ B. Bats might get caught in their hair.
   - ○ C. Bats eat insects.
   - ○ D. They realize that bats are not harmful.

2. **If you see a bat, you should**
   - ○ A. run
   - ○ B. call 911
   - ○ C. look, but don't touch
   - ○ D. try to pet it

3. **Which is not mentioned in the story as something bats eat?**
   - ○ A. fruit
   - ○ B. insects
   - ○ C. blood
   - ○ D. honey

4. **What does the word <u>myth</u> mean?**

   _____

5. **What is a myth that has been told about bats?**

   _____

6. **Why is it not a good idea to try to catch a bat?**

   _____

7. **Write at least three words that rhyme with <u>bat</u>.**

   _____

Total Correct _____

The Summer Plan

Every summer Juan and Anita get bored. The excitement of school getting out dies down, and Mom and Dad have to work. Juan and Anita are not allowed to leave their yard when no one else is home, so they read lots of books, play games, or play in the backyard. This summer was going to be different.

Earlier this year, Juan's second grade class made birdhouses for Mother's Day. Everyone complimented Juan on the birdhouse that he made. Not only was it built well, but he decorated it nicely too. Many neighbors had asked Mom where she bought it. She beamed with pride as she told them that her son had made it at school.

Anita had been studying about supply and demand in social studies. Her teacher taught her that when lots of people want something, and that item is not easy to come by, then people will pay more money for that product. This gave Anita an idea: She and Juan should start a business.

Juan loved the idea! Anita made posters advertising Juan's birdhouses. She put them up around the neighborhood. Juan worked away on the birdhouses in the basement. He sawed, nailed, and painted until he had three of the most beautiful birdhouses he had ever seen. Anita set up a table

in the front yard. They charged four dollars for each birdhouse.

By the end of their first day of business, Juan and Anita had sold all three birdhouses. Five other neighbors had requested that Juan make them a birdhouse too. One neighbor even offered to buy Mom's birdhouse for ten dollars. Juan and Anita told him that it wasn't for sale.

All summer long Juan made houses and Anita sold them. By the middle of the summer, both kids had saved up enough money to go to camp for the last week of summer vacation.

Camp was fun! Juan and Anita made new friends, learned how to do new things, and had lots of fun. Anita learned how to swim, and Juan learned how to pitch a tent. They both enjoyed arts and crafts days when Juan showed all of his new friends how to make birdhouses!

Reading Challenge

After reading "The Summer Plan," answer the following questions.

1. **What is the summer plan?**
   - ○ A. to read books and play games
   - ○ B. to play in the backyard
   - ○ C. to sell Mom's birdhouse
   - ○ D. to earn money by making and selling birdhouses

2. **Where did Juan learn to build birdhouses?**
   - ○ A. from his dad
   - ○ B. at school
   - ○ C. at camp
   - ○ D. from Anita

3. **What is it called when lots of people want something, and that item isn't easy to get, so people will pay more for it?**
   - ○ A. social studies
   - ○ B. raising the price
   - ○ C. supply and demand
   - ○ D. beaming with pride

4. **Place a 1, 2, 3, or 4 on the line beside each sentence to put the events in the correct sequence order.**

   _____ Anita made posters and put them up around the neighborhood.

   _____ Juan learned how to make birdhouses.

   _____ Someone offered to buy Mom's birdhouse.

   _____ Juan and Anita went to camp.

Total Correct _____

The Lonely Turtle

Frederick was a turtle who lived with his mother near the creek. The creek was full of other living creatures, but no one was Frederick's age. Day in and day out, Frederick tried to fit in with the older critters. He tried racing with the raccoons, but they were much faster than Frederick. He tried climbing trees with the possums, but turtles aren't made to climb. Frederick nearly broke his shell when he fell from one of the lower branches!

To fill his time, Frederick started painting rocks. He painted little rocks and big rocks. He painted flat rocks and round rocks. Sometimes he would paint a design, and other times he would paint pictures of other animals that lived near the creek. Frederick was so worried about finding someone just like him to play with, that he didn't notice how beautiful his paintings were. Instead of keeping the rocks, he would simply toss them into the creek.

Weeks went by where all Frederick did was paint. His mother was starting to worry about him. The more she tried to talk to Frederick, the more he ran off to paint. Talking about his feelings only upset Frederick, and he did not want his mother to see him cry.

The Lonely Turtle, continued

One afternoon, Frederick tossed his latest painted rock into the creek. He was startled when a large frog hopped out of the water onto the bank. "Watch out!" the frog yelled. "I'm sorry," said Frederick. "I didn't see you there."

"That's OK," said the frog. "I shouldn't have sneaked up on you like that. I just wanted to catch your next rock." "Why would you want to do a thing like that?" asked Frederick. "You don't know?" asked the frog. "Your work is beautiful! Every frog in the creek looks for your rocks. They are treasures."

"Really?" said Frederick. "Sure! Come with me," the frog said.

Frederick and the frog swam down the creek together. Frederick was amazed when he saw the frog's house. It was covered in rocks, Frederick's rocks! It was beautiful! The frog introduced Frederick to several of his friends. They had Frederick's painted rocks on their houses too. Everyone was happy to meet the artist they admired so much. One frog even asked Frederick for his autograph!

When Frederick got home, he told his mother the whole story. She was thrilled to see her little boy happy again, and Frederick was happy too. Frederick and his new friends spent afternoons playing in the creek and painting rocks. He was no longer a lonely turtle.

Reading Challenge

After reading "The Lonely Turtle," answer the following questions.

1. Who are the two main characters in this story?

   _____

   _____

2. What was Frederick's problem?
   - A. The raccoons were faster than he was.
   - B. He didn't have any friends his age.
   - C. He couldn't paint well.
   - D. The possums made fun of him.

3. What did Frederick do to pass the time?
   - A. He talked to his mom.
   - B. He drew pictures.
   - C. He climbed trees with the possums.
   - D. He painted rocks.

4. Why was the frog waiting in the creek?
   - A. He wanted to catch one of Frederick's rocks.
   - B. He was afraid of Frederick.
   - C. He was hiding from his friends.
   - D. He wanted to learn how to paint.

5. How do you think Frederick felt when he saw the frog's house? Why?

   _____

   _____

6. Do you think Frederick continued to paint rocks after he met the frog? Why or why not?

   _____

   _____

   _____

Total Correct _____

TWO

VENLAFAXINE HCl
EFFEXOR XR EXTENDED RELEASE CAPSULES

Please see accompanying Prescribing Information, including Boxed Warning.

...hings, blowing in the wind . . .
...moved, the other could bend.

...oted in the ground, growing tall.
...closely, the blade is so small.

...autiful, Mother Nature's gift.
...t climb, one you could lift.

Green is their color, brought on
by the spring.

Leaves or blades, they both
make me sing!

Name .... **Date** ....

1. What two things is the poem comparing?

   _____

2. What color are the things in the poem?

   _____

3. Find two pairs of rhyming words in the poem and write them on the lines below.

   _____

   _____

4. How does the poet feel about what she is writing?

   _____

   _____

   _____

   _____

5. How do you feel about the poem? Why?

   _____

   _____

   _____

   _____

Total Correct _____

Marvin the Moose

Marvin was a happy moose. He lived in the woods in Acadia National Park just outside Bar Harbor, Maine. Summer was Marvin's favorite time of year. From his favorite mountain, he could watch the tourists biking or watch the sailboats sailing into the harbor.

Marvin spent most of his time alone. His parents had warned him about how dangerous humans can be, and Marvin knew that it was best to stay out of their sight. However, his curiosity about the tourists in the town of Bar Harbor was just too much. Marvin longed to look into the shop windows and walk through the park of picnickers. He even dreamed about going on a whale watching cruise!

Knowing that it was unsafe to wander into town in broad daylight, Marvin decided to give it a try at night. When he heard the town clock chime ten, Marvin began his journey into Bar Harbor. He peeked into the ice cream shop where there was a young man mopping the floor. He wandered past the jewelry shop admiring the sparkles and colors. Before he knew it, Marvin had walked right onto the pier where many of the cruise ships docked.

Marvin admired the beauty of the Atlantic Ocean from the dock. He thought he could see a whale in the distance. Just below, several lobsters crawled along the sand.

Marvin was beginning to get tired. It was midnight. He decided that he was lucky that no one had spotted him and that he had better head back home. Slowly, Marvin journeyed back up the mountain and into the woods.

Marvin was very proud of himself for being so sneaky. "I walked all through town, and no one saw me!" Marvin thought. Marvin had sweet dreams as the town below was getting ready for a new day. The next morning, the paper carrier was delivering papers with a headline that read, "Moose Wanders Bar Harbor," and guess whose picture was on the front page. Shh . . . don't tell.

Reading Challenge

After reading "Marvin the Moose," answer the following questions.

Use complete sentences to answer questions 1–6.

1. Why was summer Marvin's favorite time of year?

   _____

2. Which word in the second paragraph means "wanted very badly"?

   _____

3. Did anyone see Marvin? Circle one: <u>Yes</u>   <u>No</u>   How do you know?

   _____

4. Whose picture was on the front page of the paper?

   _____

5. Why did Marvin's parents tell him to be careful around people?

   _____

6. How long was Marvin in town?

   _____

7. Place a 1, 2, 3, or 4 on the line beside each sentence to put the events in the correct order.

   _____ Marvin saw a man mopping the floor.

   _____ Marvin wandered into Bar Harbor at night.

   _____ The paper carrier delivered the morning paper.

   _____ Marvin saw the Atlantic Ocean from the dock.

Total Correct _____

Lizzy's Song

Lizzy was looking forward to trying out for the second grade play. For weeks and weeks she practiced all of her lines in front of the mirror. The play had two main parts, a deer and a butterfly. Lizzy wanted the part of the butterfly.

Tryouts were on Friday. Thursday night Lizzy had a hard time going to sleep. "What if I forget my lines?" she asked herself. Finally, Friday arrived. After lunch, all of the students who wanted to try out for the play were asked to go to the auditorium. Jennifer went first. She wanted to be the deer. She did a great job. Lizzy hoped that she would do as well as Jennifer. Next, it was Albert's turn. He was trying out for the butterfly role. Albert did a great job too. Now it was Lizzy's turn. She walked up onto the stage. Mrs. Mayfield, the music teacher, asked her to say her lines. Lizzy was speechless. She could not say a word. Her mouth was dry, and she felt sick. Lizzy had stage fright!

When Lizzy got home she cried as she told her parents what had happened. Her mother told her that when she was a little girl, she used to be afraid to talk in front of people too. Lizzy was relieved to hear that she was not the only one with stage fright.

Lizzy's Song, continued

The next day, Mrs. Mayfield gave out parts in the play. Jennifer got the part of the deer. Albert got the butterfly. Lizzy's role was a violet. All that practicing, and Lizzy had to be a flower in the school play. She was very disappointed.

Lizzy's main job was to hold the welcome sign at the edge of the stage. She did not have any lines. Even though her grandmother made her a beautiful violet costume, Lizzy was not excited when it was time for the play. "Why do I have to go?" she asked her parents. "All of the other kids have lines. The audience will laugh at me." Lizzy's parents reminded her that all of the parts in the play were important.

The night of the play, Lizzy got in her spot early. She decided that she was going to be the best violet the school had ever seen. She smiled throughout the play. At the end of the play, Allison, the narrator, was supposed to come out onto the stage and thank everyone for coming. However, Allison was nowhere to be found!

Out of the corner of her eye, Lizzy noticed Mrs. Mayfield waving at her. She seemed to be trying to tell her something. Lizzy realized that Mrs. Mayfield was trying to tell her to thank the audience. Before she realized

what she was doing, Lizzy began singing out loud. She was singing, "Good night, thank you for coming. Good night, we hope you enjoyed the show. Good night, we thank you all for coming. Good-bye, it's time for you to go!"

Everyone clapped and cheered. They loved Lizzy's song and thought it was a wonderful way to end the play. Mrs. Mayfield thought that Lizzy did such a great job that she asked her to sing the same ending for the rest of the shows.

Lizzy realized that when she sang on stage, she was not as frightened as when she tried to talk. She ended each show with her song and even added on a little dance for the last performance. Being a flower was not a bad thing after all.

Reading Challenge

After reading "Lizzy's Song," answer the following questions.

1. What part did Lizzy want in the play?
- ○ A. the violet
- ○ B. the deer
- ○ C. the butterfly
- ○ D. the narrator

2. Why didn't Lizzy get the part she wanted?
- ○ A. She yelled her lines.
- ○ B. She had stage fright.
- ○ C. She didn't practice for her part.
- ○ D. She couldn't sleep the night before tryouts.

3. Why wasn't Lizzy excited the night of the play?
- ○ A. She did not like her costume.
- ○ B. She did not know her lines.
- ○ C. She was mad at Jennifer and Albert.
- ○ D. She was afraid that people would laugh at her.

4. Why was Mrs. Mayfield waving at Lizzy?
- ○ A. She wanted Lizzy to thank the audience.
- ○ B. She wanted Lizzy to smile for the camera.
- ○ C. She wanted to say hello to Lizzy.
- ○ D. She was trying to tell Lizzy to hold up her sign.

Use complete sentences to answer the following questions.

5. What did Lizzy do at the end of the play?

_____

_____

6. Do you think Lizzy will be in other plays? Why or why not?

_____

_____

Total Correct _____

Nikki the Dog

Nikki was a black poodle. She was an only dog, with no brothers or sisters. Nikki lived with a family. There was a mother, a father, and two little girls. Nikki loved being the only pet the little girls had to play with. She got all of the attention a dog could ever want.

One day Nikki's biggest fear came true. The father of the family brought home a new puppy. He told his family that he had seen the dog on the side of the road when he was driving home from work. The puppy looked so hungry and scared, he had to bring it home.

At first Nikki growled and barked at the new dog. But when the little girls saw Nikki do that, Nikki was scolded and sent to her kennel. Nikki felt like everyone loved the new puppy more than they loved her. She curled up on her bed and cried her eyes out.

The next day, Nikki decided that she would run away. She would find a new family that loved her. She did not want to watch the new puppy get all of the love and attention from her family. She started her journey by digging a hole under the fence in the backyard. After she tunneled her way out, she started down the road.

Nikki had never been near a road without her leash on. It was very scary! Cars drove by very fast. Many of them made loud noises that frightened Nikki. She decided to get off the road and walked into the woods. After a while, Nikki realized that she did not know the way home. She was lost!

She tried going one way, but it did not look right. So she turned around and went the other way, but it did not look right either. Nikki was

Nikki the Dog, continued

tired and hungry. She didn't know what to do. She lay down to rest.

A few minutes into her nap, Nikki saw a large hound dog sniffing his way through the woods. Nikki called out to the dog. When the hound dog asked her what was wrong, Nikki told him the whole story about the new puppy and getting lost while trying to run away. The hound dog told Nikki that he had been a stray dog without a family to love him his whole life.

Talking to the hound dog helped Nikki realize that she had been a little selfish by not giving the new puppy a chance. The hound dog helped Nikki find her way back to the edge of the woods. The sun was beginning to set when the two dogs found the road. Just then, they heard someone coming. It was Nikki's family. They had been searching for her all day.

Nikki was so happy to see her family that she didn't even notice that the new puppy was leading the group trying to find her. Nikki and the new puppy became friends. The family brought the hound dog home too. The family and the dogs were all happy!

Reading Challenge

After reading "Nikki the Dog," answer the following questions.

1. **Place the numbers 1–6 on the lines beside each sentence to put the events in the correct order.**

   _____ Nikki ran away.

   _____ Nikki barked and growled at the new puppy.

   _____ The hound dog got a new home.

   _____ Nikki was an only dog.

   _____ Dad brought home a surprise.

   _____ The hound dog helped Nikki.

2. **How did Nikki get out?**
   - A. She sneaked out the door when Dad came home.
   - B. She hid in Mom's bag.
   - C. She dug a hole under the fence.
   - D. She crawled out the window.

3. **Why was Nikki sad?**
   - A. She wanted to play with the new puppy.
   - B. She had never been off her leash near a road before.
   - C. She thought everyone loved the new puppy more than her.
   - D. She didn't have any friends.

4. **Who was leading the group trying to find Nikki?**
   - A. Dad
   - B. the new puppy
   - C. the hound dog
   - D. the little girl

5. **The hound dog helped Nikki realize how lucky she was.**
   - A. true
   - B. false

6. **The family had _____ dogs at the end of the story.**
   - A. one
   - B. two
   - C. three

Total Correct _____

Lemonade

Emily Ann wanted a new pair of skates. It was several months until her next birthday, and she did not have enough money saved up from her chores to buy them. She asked her mom and dad for ideas. Mom told her that she could do some extra chores around the house to earn a few dollars, and Dad told her that her old skates were just fine. He thought she could wait until her next birthday and ask for a pair then.

Emily Ann was thinking about her parents' suggestions as she walked to her friend Stephanie's house. Stephanie lived in the same neighborhood, two streets down from Emily Ann. The first person Emily Ann saw on her walk was Mr. Smith. Mr. Smith was working in his yard. He waved to Emily Ann, then took a drink from his garden hose.

At the next intersection, where Elm Street and Peddle Drive crossed, Emily Ann saw Mr. and Mrs. Tredwell going for a jog. "Hello Emily Ann," Mrs. Tredwell called. "It's a warm day isn't it?" Emily Ann agreed.

Emily Ann walked up Stephanie's driveway. She had to walk around Stephanie's bike to get to the front door. "Hi, Stephanie!" Emily Ann called. "Why is your bike in the middle of the driveway?" "Hi, Emily Ann. I was so hot and thirsty that I had to run in to get a drink before you got here."

Emily Ann had an idea. Everyone she passed on the way to Stephanie's house seemed hot and thirsty. Maybe she could make some money to buy her skates by selling lemonade to the neighbors. She shared her idea with Stephanie, and they decided to be partners and open a lemonade stand.

They picked a corner between their houses to set up the stand. They thought an intersection would be a good place. They also decorated signs and put them up around the neighborhood. Stephanie brought lemons and cups from her house, and Emily Ann brought sugar, water, and ice from her house. Together they made the best lemonade any of the neighbors had ever had. Mr. Smith, the Tredwells, and several other neighbors came to buy lemonade from the girls. Some people even came back for seconds!

Before they knew it, it was dinnertime. The girls cleaned up their stand and counted their money. They were surprised at how much they had earned. Emily Ann had made enough in one day to buy her skates!

That night at bedtime, Emily Ann's parents came in to tuck her in. "We are so proud of you, honey," Mom said. "Just remember, you can do anything you want to do if you put your mind to it." Emily Ann smiled and closed her eyes. She knew they were right. If you try your best and use your head, you can make your dreams come true.

Reading Challenge

After reading "Lemonade," answer the following questions.

1. **What was Emily Ann's dream?**
   - ○ A. She wished that she was older.
   - ○ B. She was hot and tired.
   - ○ C. She didn't know how to make lemonade.
   - ○ D. She wanted new skates.

2. **What did Mom suggest when Emily Ann told her what she wanted?**
   - ○ A. She told her to wait until her birthday.
   - ○ B. She told her to do extra chores around the house.
   - ○ C. She told her to take a nap.
   - ○ D. She told her to make lemonade.

3. **How did Emily Ann solve her problem?**
   - ○ A. She sold lemonade.
   - ○ B. She did nothing.
   - ○ C. She went to talk to Mr. Smith.
   - ○ D. She went to her friend Stephanie's house.

4. **What word in the third paragraph means "a place where two streets cross"?**

   _____

5. **Why was this day a good day to sell lemonade?**

   _____

6. **What do you think Stephanie did with her money?**

   _____

   _____

   _____

   Total Correct _____

The Rain

Pitter patter pitter pat . . .
How I love the rain!

It's not here yet,
but I can tell it is near.

Tiny sprinkles on my face
as I walk in the morning light.

Pitter patter pitter pat . . .
How I love to feel the rain!

Tap tap tapping
on my window and door.

Pitter patter pitter pat . . .
How I love to hear the rain!

I sit at my window
and watch it come down.

Pitter patter pitter pat . . .
How I love to see the rain!

Pitter patter pitter pat . . .
How I love to smell the rain!

Pitter patter pitter pat . . .
How I love the rain!

Reading Challenge

After reading "The Rain," answer the following questions.

1. **What sense does the author not refer to in the poem?**
   - ○ A. smell
   - ○ B. taste
   - ○ C. sight
   - ○ D. hearing

2. **Where does the poet feel the rain?**
   - ○ A. on her hands
   - ○ B. on her hair
   - ○ C. on her face
   - ○ D. on her feet

3. **Does the author like rain?**
   - ○ A. yes
   - ○ B. no

4. **What phrase is repeated in this poem?**

   _____

5. **How do you feel about rain? Why?**

   _____

   _____

   _____

   _____

   _____

   _____

Total Correct _____

INSECTS

Do you know how to tell if something is an insect or not? Many people get insects and spiders mixed up. Here are a few hints to help you identify an insect when you see one. All insects have three main body parts. They have a head, a thorax (what some people call a body), and an abdomen. You can also pick out an insect by the number of legs it has. Count the legs of the next bug you spot. If it has eight legs, it isn't an insect at all, it is a spider. Insects have six legs.

Many insects go through different life stages. The technical word for going through these stages is metamorphosis. You probably know that a caterpillar turns into a butterfly, but did you know that it was an egg before it was a caterpillar?

Picture a beetle in your mind. What do you think of? Did you know that beetles start off as eggs too? Then they become mealworms. The mealworms go into what is called a pupa stage. This is much like the chrysalis for the caterpillar. The pupa does not move at all. Most who see it will think it is not alive, but the pupa is changing and growing inside of its protective cover, and it remains in one spot to do this. When it is fully grown, the beetle comes out of the hard layer that has been protecting it.

Next time you see an insect, take a second look. Find out what it is and look for interesting things about that creature.

Reading Challenge

After reading "Insects," answer the following questions.

1. How many body parts does an insect have?
   - ○ A. 1
   - ○ B. 2
   - ○ C. 3
   - ○ D. 5

2. What does metamorphosis mean?

   _____

   _____

   _____

3. How many legs does a spider have?
   - ○ A. 8
   - ○ B. 6
   - ○ C. 4
   - ○ D. 2

4. Why doesn't the pupa move at all?
   - ○ A. It is asleep.
   - ○ B. It is changing inside its protective covering.
   - ○ C. It is not alive.
   - ○ D. It is changing from an insect into a spider.

5. Which was not mentioned as a stage in a beetle's life?
   - ○ A. egg
   - ○ B. beetle
   - ○ C. pupa
   - ○ D. baby

Total Correct _____

The Pumpkin Patch

Latika's class went on a field trip to a pumpkin patch. Getting there was fun because there was so much to look at through the bus window. The leaves on the trees were so pretty. They had started to change colors. Before Latika knew it, they had arrived at the pumpkin patch.

First, the class walked through the barn. The farmer showed the students some of his farm equipment and told them what it was used for. Latika's favorite piece of equipment was the tractor. She wished that she could take it for a ride.

After touring the barn, everyone got to go for a hayride! A big, green tractor, like the one in the barn, pulled a large cart full of hay. The class had fun tossing hay into the air.

The last thing the class did was pick out a pumpkin. Each student got to take home one pumpkin. Evan picked a big, round pumpkin. Stewart chose a tall, skinny pumpkin. Latika took her time looking over the pumpkins before she picked one. Finally, she decided on a very small, round pumpkin. She thought it would look nice on the windowsill in her kitchen.

Reading Challenge

After reading "The Pumpkin Patch," answer the following questions.

1. **Place the numbers 1–5 on the lines beside each sentence to put the events in the correct order.**

   _____ Everyone picked out a pumpkin.

   _____ Latika enjoyed looking at the pretty leaves out the window.

   _____ The class went on a hayride.

   _____ The class took a tour of the barn.

   _____ They arrived at the pumpkin patch.

2. **What season was it when Latika's class went on the field trip?**
   ○ A. winter
   ○ B. spring
   ○ C. summer
   ○ D. fall

3. **What was Latika's favorite tool in the barn?**
   ○ A. a cart
   ○ B. the tractor
   ○ C. the pitchfork
   ○ D. a plow

4. **Which is not something that the story tells us Latika's class did?**
   ○ A. picked out pumpkins
   ○ B. walked through the barn
   ○ C. played on the tractor
   ○ D. went on a hayride

5. **Ride and decide are words that have the long i (ī)sound. Which word below does not have the long i (ī) sound?**
   ○ A. big
   ○ B. fly
   ○ C. hide
   ○ D. tie

Total Correct _____

The Koala

Have you ever seen a koala? If you have been to Australia, you probably have. That is where koalas live. You can find them eating leaves from a special kind of tree called a eucalyptus tree.

Many people think koalas are bears because they look cute and cuddly like a bear cub. Koalas are not bears. They are marsupials.

Marsupials are special kinds of mammals. Like other mammals, they have fur, have babies instead of laying eggs, and they get milk from their mothers. Koalas, like other marsupials, have a pouch where their babies go to stay warm and safe.

After reading "The Koala," answer the following questions.

1. **Where do koalas live?**
   - A. in the woods
   - B. in Australia
   - C. in South America
   - D. in a house

2. **What do koalas eat?**
   - A. hamburgers
   - B. fruit
   - C. cranberry leaves
   - D. eucalyptus leaves

3. **Which is not true of mammals?**
   - A. They have fur.
   - B. They have webbed feet.
   - C. They have babies instead of laying eggs.
   - D. They get milk from their mothers.

4. **What makes marsupials different from other mammals?**
   - A. They have a pouch.
   - B. They eat leaves.
   - C. They get milk from their mothers.
   - D. They have fur.

5. **Why do some people think koalas are bears?**
   - A. They sound like bears.
   - B. They are marsupials.
   - C. They are cute and cuddly.
   - D. They live in the woods.

Total Correct _____

Costume Party

Katie and Jenny were going to a costume party. Both girls were having trouble deciding what to wear. Katie wanted to be a pirate, but she knew that Fred was already planning to dress like a pirate. Jenny thought that she would put several purple balloons together and go as a bunch of grapes, but then she realized that she would have trouble sitting down without popping her costume.

The girls were talking about their problem on the playground. They made lots of suggestions to each other, but for one reason or another, nothing sounded like a good idea. Some of the other students in their class came by and told Katie and Jenny what they planned to be, and that only made the girls wonder more.

Later that night, Jenny was cleaning up her room. While she was putting her shoes away in the closet, she saw something that gave her an idea.

Last summer, for the camp play, Jenny and another friend dressed up like a horse. Jenny's grandmother had made a costume that the girls wore together. Jenny called Katie to see what she thought of going to the costume party together, as the horse.

The girls didn't tell anyone what their costume was going to be. When they came into the party as a big horse, everyone laughed. At first no one knew who was dressed in the horse costume, but when prizes were given out for the best costumes, Katie and Jenny uncovered their faces when they went to get their first place ribbon!

Reading Challenge

After reading "Costume Party," answer the following questions.

1. **What was troubling Katie and Jenny?**
   - ○ A. They were not invited to the costume party.
   - ○ B. They couldn't decide what to wear to the costume party.
   - ○ C. They weren't getting along with each other.
   - ○ D. They had to clean up their rooms.

2. **Which is not a costume either of the girls thought about wearing?**
   - ○ A. grapes
   - ○ B. pirate
   - ○ C. bunny
   - ○ D. horse

3. **How did Jenny get the idea that she and Katie used for a costume?**
   - ○ A. Katie told her what they should be.
   - ○ B. Her grandmother gave her the idea.
   - ○ C. She saw an old costume in her closet.
   - ○ D. Fred gave her a suggestion.

4. **Which word below could replace the name <u>Fred</u> in the following sentence: Fred was going to be a pirate.**
   - ○ A. He
   - ○ B. They
   - ○ C. She
   - ○ D. It

5. **Did the other children like Jenny and Katie's costume?**
   - ○ A. no
   - ○ B. yes

6. **What happens in the story to prove your answer to number 5 above?**

   _____

   _____

   _____

Total Correct _____

Rudy Gets Lost

Mother sent Rudy Raccoon to get some corn for their family supper. Just as Rudy was picking the last ear that he needed, it began to rain. He was on his way home when he realized that he was lost.

Rudy went to the edge of the cornfield to try to retrace his steps. This was hard to do because it was hard to see in the rain. Next he decided that he would follow his footprints. This seemed like a good idea, except the rain had washed away any prints that Rudy had left in the dirt.

Rudy was just about to give up when he remembered that his friend Moe Mole lived at the edge of the cornfield. Rudy decided to ask Moe for help. After a good bit of looking around, Rudy found the entrance to Moe's burrow.

Moe was delighted to see Rudy. He invited Rudy in for some juice and crackers. Rudy told Moe his problem while he dried off by the fire.

Soon the rain stopped, and Moe

Rudy Gets Lost, continued

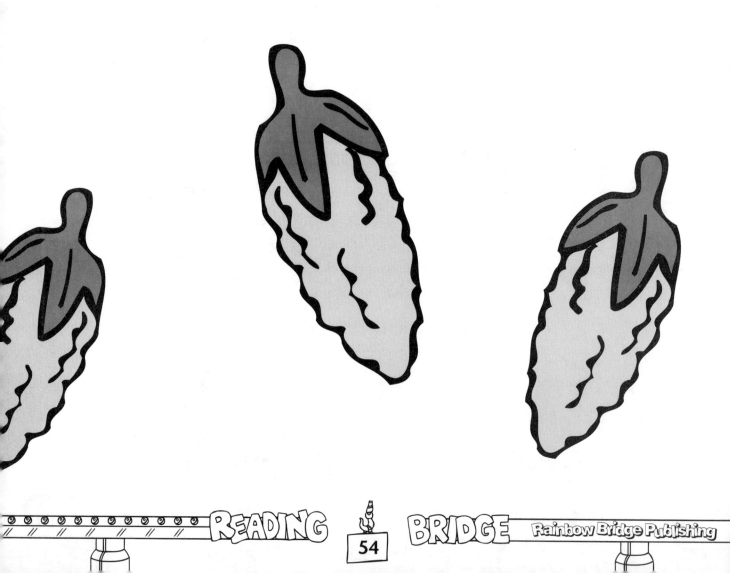

and Rudy went back out to try to find their way to Rudy's house. Moe led the way. He had terrible eyesight, but he had a wonderful sense of smell. Moe sniffed here and there until he knew which way to go. Before they knew it, they were back at Rudy's house.

Mother was so happy to see Rudy. She had started to worry when the rain began. The Raccoons invited Moe Mole to stay for dinner. They all enjoyed a delicious meal. Everyone agreed that the corn was the best part.

Reading Challenge

After reading "Rudy Gets Lost," answer the following questions.

1. **Why was Rudy in the cornfield?**
   - ○ A. He was playing hide-and-seek.
   - ○ B. Mom sent him to get corn for supper.
   - ○ C. He was going to visit his friend Moe Mole.
   - ○ D. Rudy is a farmer.

2. **What was Rudy's situation?**
   - ○ A. He was lost.
   - ○ B. He couldn't see well.
   - ○ C. He couldn't find enough corn.
   - ○ D. He got wet.

3. **Which was not something Rudy tried to do to fix his problem?**
   - ○ A. He tried to retrace his steps.
   - ○ B. He went to his friend for help.
   - ○ C. He tried to follow his footprints.
   - ○ D. He called out for help.

4. **Mother and Rudy are two words from the story that have two syllables, or beats. Which word below also has two syllables?**
   - ○ A. wonderful
   - ○ B. last
   - ○ C. started
   - ○ D. remembered

5. **Place the numbers 1–5 on the lines beside each sentence to put the events in the correct order.**

   _____ It started to rain.

   _____ Moe Mole helped Rudy.

   _____ Everyone enjoyed a delicious dinner.

   _____ Rudy tried to follow his footprints.

   _____ Mother sent Rudy to get some corn.

Total Correct _____

Teddy

Mom and Dad think I'm too old

to still have my teddy bear.

They say, "You are eight years old now,

and Teddy shows too much wear."

I nod my head and then agree.

I know I'm a real strong kid.

Without a thought I put him up,

and in my closet he hid.

That same night, I tried and tried,

but could not fall asleep.

A storm came in with lots of noise.

I did not make a peep.

Instead, I took my bear out

of the hiding place I made.

I did not need him to fall asleep.

I just knew he was afraid.

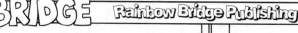

Reading Challenge

After reading "Teddy," answer the following questions.

1. **Why do the parents want the child to put the teddy bear away?**
   - ○ A. They think the child is too old to have a teddy bear.
   - ○ B. They think that the child will lose the bear.
   - ○ C. They want the child to play with other toys.
   - ○ D. They think teddy bears are silly.

2. **Why couldn't the child in the poem fall asleep?**
   - ○ A. The child was cold.
   - ○ B. The child was worried that Mom and Dad were angry.
   - ○ C. The child was hungry.
   - ○ D. The child thought the teddy bear was afraid.

3. **What did the child do when there was a storm?**
   - ○ A. went into Mom and Dad's room
   - ○ B. got the teddy bear
   - ○ C. cried
   - ○ D. hid under the covers

4. **Kid and hid are words that rhyme in the poem. Which two words in the pairs below do not rhyme?**
   - ○ A. fun and run
   - ○ B. bike and ride
   - ○ C. bear and tear
   - ○ D. hide and side

5. **Asleep and peep are words in the poem that make the long e (ē) sound. Which word below does not have the long e (ē) sound?**
   - ○ A. read
   - ○ B. see
   - ○ C. agree
   - ○ D. bed

Total Correct _____

GERMS

Have you ever heard someone ask you to please cover your mouth when you sneeze or cough? Do you know why you should do that? It is to keep germs that you have from spreading to other people. Germs are not something we can see, but when they get into our bodies, they can make us sick. Germs can travel in lots of ways.

Some of the most common ways germs can get into your body are through your nose, mouth, eyes, and cuts in your skin. Many people don't know that one of the most common ways that germs can cause colds is through a person's eyes. That's why you don't want to rub your eyes.

There are lots of ways to protect your body from germs. You should wash your hands with soap several times a day, especially before meals and after using the bathroom. It is also smart to keep your own germs to yourself. You can do this by covering your mouth when you cough or sneeze, not sharing your food or drink with others, and by keeping your fingers out of your nose or mouth.

Staying healthy can help keep germs away too. It is important to get exercise every day. Eating healthy meals can also help. If you skip meals, your body gets weak and cannot fight off the germs that do get in. Getting a good night's sleep will also help you stay strong and healthy.

Reading Challenge

After reading "Germs," answer the following questions.

1. Which is <u>not</u> a way germs get into your body.
   - ○ A. through your eyes
   - ○ B. through cuts in your skin
   - ○ C. through your nose
   - ○ D. by washing your hands

2. Which is <u>not</u> a way to protect your body from germs?
   - ○ A. Eat lots of junk food.
   - ○ B. Get a good night's sleep.
   - ○ C. Wash your hands with soap.
   - ○ D. Keep your fingers out of your nose and mouth.

3. We can see germs.
   - ○ A. true
   - ○ B. false

4. Write the following words in alphabetical order.

   | germs | mouth | sick |
   | sneeze | eyes | |

   _____

   _____

5. <u>Sunshine</u> is a compound word. <u>Sun</u> + <u>shine</u> = <u>sunshine</u>. Use the following words to make at least three more compound words.

   | rain | fly | horse | back |
   | drop | saw | dew | |

   _____

   _____

   _____

   _____

   _____

Total Correct _____

Ed and Emily

Ed and Emily had been best friends since kindergarten. They were next-door neighbors and had been in the same class at school for three years. They rode bikes to school together every morning and home again every afternoon. So Ed was surprised when Emily wasn't waiting for him on Friday afternoon.

Ed rode home as fast as he could. He left his bike in the driveway and ran inside. He called Emily's house and asked her mom if she could come out to play. Emily's mom told Ed that she thought Emily was in the back-

yard, so Ed headed over that way. He looked all over the yard, but he couldn't find Emily anywhere. He decided to check the clubhouse to see if he could see her from there.

As he was climbing the rope ladder, Ed heard voices. One was Emily's, but he wasn't sure who the other voice belonged to. When he poked his head through the clubhouse entrance, he saw Emily and Margaret Ellsworth, a girl that went to his school. "Hi!" Ed said, "Why didn't you answer when I called you?"

"Because," said Margaret, "this is a girls only club, and you can't be a member. No boys are allowed in this clubhouse, so you better climb down." Ed looked at Emily, knowing that she would explain to Margaret that this was their clubhouse. Of course boys were allowed. Emily didn't say a word. She just shrugged her shoulders and looked down at her feet.

The next morning, Ed asked Mom to drive him to school. He didn't feel much like riding his bike. He didn't look at Emily all day long. At lunch, he ate with some other boys. He hid on the playground all of recess. When Emily came over to Ed's house after school, Ed told his mom to tell her to go away. Emily told Ed's mom what happened the day before and asked if she could come in and talk to Ed.

Ed turned his back on Emily when she walked into his room. "Didn't Mom tell you?" he said. "I don't feel like playing." "I came over to say I'm sorry," Emily said. "I should not have let Margaret talk to you that way. I'm sorry." Ed asked, "Why didn't you tell her that it was our clubhouse? Why didn't you tell her that I could play, too?" "I wanted Margaret to like me," Emily said. "You are my best friend, Ed, but it is good to have other friends too. Margaret is the only girl I have had over all year. I didn't want to lose her as a friend. However, I thought about it last night, and I decided that I don't want to be friends with someone who is going to be mean to my best friend. So I told Margaret today that you are welcome in the play-house. I invited her over again this Saturday. Let's give her another chance."

Ed agreed to give Margaret a second chance, and Emily agreed to stand up for Ed. Now, Emily and Ed were both looking forward to Saturday.

Reading Challenge

After reading "Ed and Emily," answer the following questions.

1. **What surprised Ed after school?**
   - ○ A. His bike was missing.
   - ○ B. A dog jumped out in front of him.
   - ○ C. It was raining.
   - ○ D. Emily wasn't waiting for him.

2. **What did Emily do when Margaret was mean to Ed?**
   - ○ A. She stood up for Ed.
   - ○ B. She did not say anything.
   - ○ C. She said mean things to Ed, too.
   - ○ D. She cried.

3. **Why did Ed ride to school with Mom the next day?**
   - ○ A. It was raining.
   - ○ B. His feelings were hurt.
   - ○ C. His bike tire was flat.
   - ○ D. He couldn't find his bike.

4. **How did Emily fix her friendship with Ed?**
   - ○ A. She told Ed that she would not play with Margaret anymore.
   - ○ B. She stayed away from Ed and Margaret.
   - ○ C. She said she was sorry and invited Ed to play on Saturday.
   - ○ D. She made some new friends.

5. **Where was Emily when Ed was looking for her?**
   - ○ A. in the clubhouse
   - ○ B. down the street
   - ○ C. on the playground
   - ○ D. at the park

6. **Place the numbers 1–6 on the lines beside each sentence to put the events in the correct order.**

   _____ Ed found Margaret and Emily.

   _____ Ed and Emily were in kindergarten together.

   _____ Emily left school without Ed.

   _____ Margaret was mean to Ed.

   _____ Emily tried to fix the problem.

   _____ Ed hid at recess.

Total Correct _____

Nana's Gift

Elizabeth was scared. She had been waiting in the hospital waiting room ever since school got out. When she got off the bus, she knew something was wrong when Mrs. Brady, her neighbor, picked her up after school instead of her mom.

Mrs. Brady explained to Elizabeth that her mom and dad were at the hospital with Elizabeth's grandmother, Nana. She told Elizabeth that Nana had a medical problem called a stroke.

When they got to the hospital, Elizabeth's dad met them in the waiting room and told them that Nana was still with the doctor. He promised that he would come back as soon as he had any news.

Finally, Elizabeth's dad came back. He told Elizabeth that Nana was going to be okay. She would have to stay in the hospital a few days. Then she would be living with their family while she got better.

Elizabeth couldn't wait for her grandmother to come stay with them. She made a sign that said "Welcome Home!" Then she put some of her favorite stuffed animals in Nana's new room.

Nana's stroke caused her to forget how to do lots of things. She had trouble walking and talking. Elizabeth helped Nana every day. Sometimes they would go for a walk. Elizabeth held Nana's hand, and they walked very slowly.

Sometimes Elizabeth would read with Nana. Nana needed lots of help with reading, so Elizabeth taught her how to sound out the words. They would take turns. Elizabeth would read a few pages, then Nana would read a sentence or two. Then it would be Elizabeth's turn again.

Elizabeth would never forget the day she turned eight. When she got home from school, Mom told her that Nana wanted to see her in her room. Elizabeth sat on Nana's bed, and Nana opened her book. Elizabeth cried as she listened to Nana read the whole story all by herself. Elizabeth was so happy for her. Nana had been working so hard, and now she had done it! She had learned to read again! It was the best birthday Elizabeth had ever had!

Reading Challenge

After reading "Nana's Gift," answer the following questions.

1. **Why did Mrs. Brady pick Elizabeth up from the bus instead of Mom?**
   - ○ A. Mom was working late.
   - ○ B. Mom and Dad were out of town.
   - ○ C. Elizabeth's family was at the hospital.
   - ○ D. She was taking Elizabeth to soccer practice.

2. **What happened to Nana?**
   - ○ A. She went on vacation.
   - ○ B. She had a stroke.
   - ○ C. She fell asleep.
   - ○ D. She twisted her ankle.

3. **Which is not something that the story tells us Elizabeth did to help Nana?**
   - ○ A. read with her
   - ○ B. went on walks with her
   - ○ C. sang her songs
   - ○ D. put some stuffed animals in Nana's room

4. **Which is something Nana did not have to learn to do again?**
   - ○ A. talk
   - ○ B. walk
   - ○ C. read
   - ○ D. see

5. **Met is a word in the story that has the short e (ĕ) sound. Which word below does not have the short e (ĕ) sound?**
   - ○ A. she
   - ○ B. net
   - ○ C. elephant
   - ○ D. red

6. **Place the numbers 1–5 on the lines beside each sentence to put the events in the correct order.**

   _____   Nana surprised Elizabeth for her birthday.

   _____   Elizabeth made a sign for Nana.

   _____   Elizabeth helped Nana walk.

   _____   Nana had to go to the hospital.

   _____   Elizabeth's dad told her what had happened.

Total Correct _____

LUCAS

Lucas is a hummingbird with a little problem. His problem wasn't that he could not fly fast. Lucas was one of the fastest hummingbirds in his neighborhood. He could drink nectar well, and he could hover in one place for over an hour! That was a record in his school. His problem was that he could not hum.

Lucas has a beautiful singing voice. He can sing all sorts of songs. Birds would come from all around to make their requests and hear Lucas sing their favorite tunes. For Lucas, not being able to hum was not even a problem until this summer.

Mrs. Teedle was the new community music director for the summer. She wanted to surprise the community with a concert at the summer celebration. She got all of the birds together to try out for different parts. Lucas went to try out, of course, because he loved to sing. Mrs. Teedle did not know Lucas, and she had never heard him sing before.

She assumed that Lucas would be a great hummer, since he was a hummingbird. She didn't even give him a

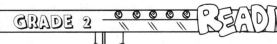

chance to try out for one of the singing parts. She just cast him as a hummer. When the group began to sing and hum their parts in the first song, everyone looked at Lucas and laughed. Lucas was not humming at all. They thought he was trying to be funny.

Lucas really wasn't trying to be funny. He couldn't hum. He was so embarrassed that he flew out of the room without saying good-bye to anyone. Some of the other birds told Mrs. Teedle how beautifully Lucas sang. She was ashamed for jumping to conclusions about Lucas. She knew better than to judge people from the outside.

Mrs. Teedle found Lucas in the city garden. She apologized to him for not giving him a chance. She asked Lucas to try out for one of the singing parts. Lucas agreed to come back the next day.

When the afternoon of the summer celebration finally arrived, the whole town was delighted with the surprise concert. Lucas had the main part. The crowd clapped and cheered, and Lucas thought, "It's great to be different."

Reading Challenge

After reading "Lucas," answer the following questions.

1. **What was Lucas's problem?**
   - ○ A. He could not fly fast.
   - ○ B. He didn't know Mrs. Teedle.
   - ○ C. He could not hum.
   - ○ D. He didn't have a very good voice.

2. **How did Mrs. Teedle surprise the community?**
   - ○ A. She held a concert at the summer celebration.
   - ○ B. She had Lucas sing in the play.
   - ○ C. She took everyone to the park.
   - ○ D. She sang a song at the summer celebration.

3. **What was Mrs. Teedle's mistake?**
   - ○ A. She laughed at Lucas.
   - ○ B. She was not very nice to the students.
   - ○ C. She picked a bad day for the concert.
   - ○ D. She jumped to conclusions about Lucas and did not give him a chance.

4. **Did Lucas give Mrs. Teedle another chance?**
   - ○ A. no
   - ○ B. yes

<u>Couldn't</u> is a contraction from the story. It is made up of the words <u>could</u> and <u>not</u>. Write the contractions for the words below.

5. it is _____

6. does not _____

7. they will_____

Total Correct _____

Who's There?

"My back hurts from the jumping boys do.
My cushion fabric used to be blue,
but now it is gray from much wear and tear.
My arms are tired from those who rest there."

"That's nothing," the next one replied.
"Try spilt soda on your top," then he sighed.
"Most people, while sitting right upon you,
put their feet on me without taking off their shoes!"

"Oh yeah," said the next, "You've both got it made.
I can see nothing from under this shade.
One minute I'm on, and the next I am not.
Quite honestly, bulbs can get really hot."

"Shhh," one says, "I hear someone coming."
Then a key turns in the slot.
Of course, when you're not there, your things don't talk!
Maybe so, maybe not . . .

Reading Challenge

After reading "Who's There?" answer the following questions.

1. What is this poem about?
- ○ A. a hurt little boy
- ○ B. pieces of furniture talking to each other
- ○ C. someone sitting on the beach
- ○ D. a child hiding from his parents

2. Who or what is "talking" in the first stanza? (A <u>stanza</u> is a group of lines in a poem, like a paragraph.)
- ○ A. a little boy
- ○ B. a dad
- ○ C. a sofa
- ○ D. a table

3. Who or what is "talking" in the third stanza?
- ○ A. a tree
- ○ B. a man
- ○ C. a table
- ○ D. a lamp

4. Is this poem realistic or fantasy?
- ○ A. fantasy
- ○ B. realistic

5. <u>Not</u> and <u>hot</u> are two words from the poem that rhyme. Which two words below do not rhyme?
- ○ A. made and shade
- ○ B. blue and do
- ○ C. shoe and you
- ○ D. den and bean

6. Who do you think is at the door at the end of the poem?

_____

Total Correct _____

AMAZING ANTS

If someone asked you to name an amazing creature, would you think to say ants? Ants are pretty terrific when you think about how long they have been around. Some types of ants have been around since the days of dinosaurs!

Ants are everywhere. The only places where you will not find ants are places where it is so cold that there is snow and ice there all year. Places like Antarctica and the Arctic do not have ants.

There are thousands of different types of ants. Most ants, however, have lots of things in common. Like other insects, ants have three main body parts: a head, a thorax, and an abdomen. Ants have feelers, called antennas, coming out of the top of their heads. These feelers are used to smell, identify other ants, and identify kinds of food.

Another tool that ants have in their mouths are their jaws, called mandibles. Many ants have very sharp teeth in these jaws. The most interesting thing about an ant's jaws is the way they open. Unlike most jaws that open up and down, an ant's jaws open sideways. They use these mandibles not only to eat, but to carry their young and to fight.

The way ants work together and how they live is interesting. Ants are also unusually strong. If you are interested in finding out more about these amazing creatures, look in your media center for articles, books, and websites that can tell you more.

Reading Challenge

After reading "Amazing Ants," answer the following questions.

1. How many different kinds of ants are there?
- ○ A. hundreds
- ○ B. thousands
- ○ C. a few
- ○ D. three

2. How many main body parts do ants have?
- ○ A. two
- ○ B. three
- ○ C. one
- ○ D. five

3. Which is not something ants use their feelers for?
- ○ A. to smell
- ○ B. to identify kinds of food
- ○ C. to identify other ants
- ○ D. to see

4. Which is not true about ants' mandibles?
- ○ A. They are used to eat.
- ○ B. Ants use them to fight.
- ○ C. They open up and down.
- ○ D. Ants carry their young with them.

5. Ants are strong.
- ○ A. true
- ○ B. false

For questions 6 and 7, write F if the statement is a fact. Write O if the statement is an opinion.

6. Ants are amazing. _____

7. Ants have been around a long time. _____

Total Correct _____

Sea Dreams

Kathleen decided to be a marine biologist when she was a little girl. She has always loved the water, and learning about plant and animal life in the sea was fun for her. She remembers the day that she decided what she wanted to be when she grew up.

It was a warm summer day, and Kathleen was about seven years old. Her family was spending the summer with their cousins on Pawley's Island in South Carolina. Kathleen used to ride her bike to the marina to watch the boats coming in. She especially liked watching the shrimp boats empty their holds full of shrimp. Each day brought exciting new surprises. The surprise on this day was not a good one.

Kathleen noticed the crowd that was gathered next to Mr. Carlton's fishing boat. At first, she thought that Mr. Carlton had caught another prize-winning fish. Unfortunately, this was not the case. As she got closer, she noticed that the people in the crowd looked worried. Some even looked frightened. "What is everyone so upset about?" Kathleen wondered. When she got to the edge of the dock, she found out.

A giant sea turtle had become caught in Mr. Carlton's fishing net. It had struggled so much to get out that it was twisted in several different directions. Some of the ropes seemed to be hurting the turtle, and one was wrapped tightly around the turtle's neck. It looked like it was struggling to breathe. Kathleen gasped at the sight, but then she did something.

Kathleen knelt down to touch the turtle. She loosened the net that was around its front leg. Then she tried to loosen the rope around the turtle's neck. Other people tried to help, too. Mr. Carlton took out his fishing knife and cut the rope from around the turtle's neck. Kathleen thought that

she saw the turtle smile. The turtle was taken to a university biology department for medical care.

Kathleen went to visit the sea turtle several times. The university had a sea lab with marine biologists and special doctors. They were making sure the turtle got the best care until it was ready to go back to its home in the sea. One of the professors complimented Kathleen on her bravery. He told her that she should think about being a marine biologist when she grew up.

Kathleen is now grown up. It took a lot of hard work, but she is a marine biologist. She spends her time learning about and trying to protect sea life. Every time Kathleen comes across a sea turtle, she wonders if it is the same turtle that she helped save when she was a little girl.

Reading Challenge

After reading "Sea Dreams," answer the following questions.

1. What was the "surprise" the story tells us Kathleen saw when she rode up to the marina?
   - ○ A. Mr. Carlton's birthday
   - ○ B. a big fish
   - ○ C. a turtle caught in a net
   - ○ D. a brave little girl

2. Which word best describes Kathleen?
   - ○ A. shy
   - ○ B. brave
   - ○ C. silly
   - ○ D. mean

3. What does Kathleen do now that she is all grown up?
   - ○ A. She is a marine biologist.
   - ○ B. She goes fishing.
   - ○ C. She rides her bike to the marina.
   - ○ D. She talks to turtles.

Win is the root or base word of the word winning. For questions 4–6, write the root or base word for these other words from the story.

4. wanted _____

5. fishing _____

6. watching _____

7. looked _____

8. twisted _____

9. Do you think Kathleen ever saw the same turtle again? Why or why not?

_____

_____

Total Correct _____

Americans in History

Our country, the United States of America, is more than two hundred years old. We celebrate our country's birthday each year on the Fourth of July, or Independence Day. Many people celebrate this special holiday with a parade, picnics, and fireworks. Independence Day is a good time to think about Americans in history who helped our country. Two important Americans were George Washington and Thomas Jefferson.

George Washington was our first president. He led many battles. There is a legend about George Washington as a little boy. It was said that he could not tell a lie. The story says little George cut down a cherry tree. When he was asked if he did it, he tried to lie, but he could not. George Washington was an honest man. Maybe that is why

Americans in History, _{continued}

he was chosen to be on the one-dollar bill.

Thomas Jefferson was another president. In 1776, Jefferson wrote the Declaration of Independence that helped start the United States. He became the third president of the United States in 1801.

Reading Challenge

After reading "Americans in History," answer the following questions.

1. **How old is the United States of America?**
   - ○ A. more than two hundred years
   - ○ B. one hundred years
   - ○ C. over two thousand years
   - ○ D. fifty years

2. **What is another name for Independence Day?**
   - ○ A. Presidents' Day
   - ○ B. Memorial Day
   - ○ C. Fourth-of-July
   - ○ D. The Declaration of Independence

3. **What did Thomas Jefferson do in 1776?**
   - ○ A. He wrote the Declaration of independence.
   - ○ B. He became President.
   - ○ C. He made the first dollar bill.
   - ○ D. He rang the Liberty Bell.

4. **Where does the story tell us we can find a picture of George Washington?**

   _____

5. **What does the story tell us that George Washington could not do?**
   - ○ A. cook pancakes
   - ○ B. tell a lie
   - ○ C. lead battles
   - ○ D. be president

Total Correct _____

A Little Brother

Bridger is in the second grade. He likes to play soccer and collect trading cards. Bridger likes school. He enjoys reading and has lots of friends, but the best thing about being at school is getting a break from Val.

Val is Bridger's baby brother. Val is only three years old. Sometimes he is cute, especially when he gives hugs. Having a little brother can also be a pain in the neck sometimes.

Just last week, Bridger put all of his trading cards in order in an album. It looked great. When he got home from school, he couldn't believe what he saw. Val had taken all of the cards out and spread them all over the room. He even put some of them in the toilet! The week before, Bridger was looking for his science report. He had been working on it for weeks, and it was time to turn it in. When Bridger finally found it, it was in Val's room covered in crayon scribble!

Bridger tried to talk to Mom about all of this. She explained to Bridger that Val was only three, and sometimes three-year-olds don't know any better. This did not make Bridger feel any better about his trading cards or his science report. Sometimes, Bridger wished he were still the only child.

One afternoon when he came home from school, Bridger couldn't find Mom. There was a note on the fridge that said, "Stay right here, Grandma is on her way over." Bridger got

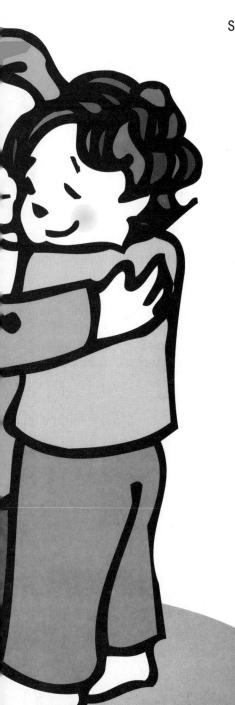

scared, so he called his dad at work. The woman who answered the phone told him that his dad just left, because there had been an emergency. She would not tell him what the emergency was. Finally, Grandma arrived. She told Bridger that Val had fallen off a chair and hit his head. He was trying to get something off one of Bridger's shelves. Val and Mom had gone to the hospital in an ambulance! Bridger was very worried. He felt terrible for being mad at Val.

Every time the phone rang, Grandma jumped up to get it. People calling to check on Val. Finally, after dark, Mom and Dad called. Val was going to be all right. He had to have a few stitches, and he was going to have a knot on his head, but he was going to be just fine. Val spent the night in the hospital.

The next day, Bridger was so happy to see his brother that he let him have some of his trading cards. He also let Val have half of his dessert after dinner. Val giggled and hugged Bridger. Bridger realized that little brothers can be a lot of trouble, but they are also important. He would try to be nice to Val from now on.

Reading Challenge

After reading "A Little Brother," answer the following questions.

1. Which is **not** something the story says Bridger likes to do?
   - ○ A. read
   - ○ B. go to school
   - ○ C. fish
   - ○ D. play soccer

2. Which is something that Val didn't do in this story?
   - ○ A. scribbled on Bridger's science report
   - ○ B. hid Bridger's homework in the closet
   - ○ C. put Bridger's trading cards in the toilet
   - ○ D. climbed on a chair to get something off a shelf

3. Talking to Mom helped Bridger feel better about the things Val was doing wrong.
   - ○ A. false
   - ○ B. true

4. Why did Bridger give Val some of his trading cards?
   - ○ A. so Val could flush them down the toilet
   - ○ B. to keep Val from telling on him
   - ○ C. to be nice in front of Mom and Dad.
   - ○ D. because Val was all right and Bridger was happy to see him.

5. Hospital is a word with three beats, or syllables. Which word below does **not** have three syllables?
   - ○ A. mosquito
   - ○ B. explained
   - ○ C. answering
   - ○ D. ambulance

Total Correct _____

Olivia's Dance

Olivia is known throughout the sea as one of the most talented creatures. She has been tap dancing for as long as she can remember. Olivia is an octopus. When you watch her tap dance, you are in for four times the show you would see if you were watching someone with only two legs. Onlookers come from oceans far, far away to see her.

Tonight was a special night for Olivia. She was dancing for King Manatee and his family. King Manatee had traveled many miles to watch Olivia dance. Princess Penelope, the king's daughter, wanted to be a dancer just like Olivia. It was Penelope's birthday wish to watch Olivia tap dance.

Usually, Olivia was quite comfortable in all of her shows. But tonight was a little different. She could not eat a bite of her dinner. When her friend Louis Lobster asked her what was wrong, she told him that she had never performed in front of royalty before. Olivia was nervous. Louis calmed her down by talking to her and keeping her company until it was time for Olivia to get dressed. But that was when the real problem began.

"Louis!" Olivia screamed from her dressing room. "There are only seven tap shoes in my

closet! I can't find my other shoe!" "Are you sure?" Louis asked. "They were all here last night when you performed for the Tuna family." "I know," replied Olivia, "I can't imagine what happened to that shoe. Oh, what should I do?"

Olivia put on her other seven shoes and gave tapping a try in her dressing room. "It's no use," she cried. "We will have to cancel the show. I can't dance with only seven shoes. It will mess up the rhythm of all the routines." Louis went out to break the bad news. Just after he left, Olivia heard a tiny voice. "Maybe I can help," the voice said. "Who said that?" Olivia asked. "It's me, Chloe." Olivia looked down to see her neighbor, Chloe Clam, peeking into her dressing room door. "I'm tiny, but I have very big ideas," Chloe said. Olivia listened to Chloe's plan.

Just in the nick of time, Chloe and Olivia caught up with Louis. "Don't cancel the show," Olivia said.

"Chloe has a plan, and I think it just might work!" They shared the idea with Louis. "Let's give it a try," he said.

Olivia danced better than she had ever danced. She was given three standing ovations, and on the third one, she spoke. "Your majesties, I must tell you what an honor it has been to dance for you. I must also let you know that I did not perform alone tonight." At that moment Olivia took something off the bottom of one of her tentacles. It was Chloe! She continued, "I would like to introduce you to my dear friend Chloe Clam. You see, I couldn't find one of my tap shoes tonight, and Chloe had a great idea. She suggested that I tape her to the bottom of one of my regular shoes. Then it would make a tapping sound just like the others. We tried it, and it worked." Chloe smiled at the princess and said, "It's a pleasure to meet you." "Likewise," said Penelope.

The king was pleased that his daughter's heroine had been able to demonstrate such teamwork. He decided to do something special for Olivia and Chloe. The king had a brand new dance studio built for Olivia to dance in. In the front row, he built a special chair, taller than the rest, for Chloe. Every year the king and his family returned for Penelope's birthday just to watch Olivia dance.

Reading Challenge

After reading "Olivia's Dance," answer the following questions.

1. **Place the numbers 1–5 on the lines beside each sentence to put the events in the correct order.**

   _____ Olivia was given three standing ovations for her show.

   _____ Olivia couldn't find one of her shoes.

   _____ Chloe, Olivia, and Penelope all became friends.

   _____ Chloe had a plan to help Olivia.

   _____ The king was pleased with Olivia and Chloe's teamwork.

2. **Why was the night in the story a special night for Olivia?**
   - A. It was her birthday.
   - B. She and Louis became friends.
   - C. She was dancing for King Manatee and his family.
   - D. She was singing a new song for the king.

3. **How did Chloe help Olivia?**
   - A. She brought her dinner on the night of her big show.
   - B. She let Olivia tape her to her shoe so it would make a tapping sound.
   - C. She helped Olivia learn her new dance routine.
   - D. She introduced Olivia to King Manatee and Princess Penelope.

4. **What did the king do for Chloe?**
   - A. He came to watch Olivia dance every year.
   - B. He built a new dance studio.
   - C. He took everyone out to dinner.
   - D. He built her a special tall chair in the front row.

5. **What do you think happened to Olivia's shoe?**

   _____

   _____

   _____

   Total Correct _____

Cameron Crow

Cameron was a young crow who lived in the trees of the Chattahoochee National Forest in Georgia. Cameron had lived in the same tree since she was born, but now her family was moving. Cameron was nervous about moving. She liked it in her forest where she had many friends.

The main thing Cameron was worried about was not being liked by the other children who lived near her new home. "No one will pick me to play on their team," Cameron whined. "Where on earth did you get such an idea?" asked Momma Crow. Cameron said, "Robin and Jay have so many colors in their feathers. They would make friends easily. Susie Songbird wouldn't have any trouble either. She has a beautiful voice. No one will want to play with me. I'm just a plain old black bird, and I can't even sing."

Momma Crow reminded Cameron of her own friends by asking, "Do you worry about what your friends look like? Don't you think it's more important how they

act and how they treat others?" Cameron knew that this was true, but still she was nervous.

Finally the time came for the Crow family to move. They said farewell to all of their friends in the forest and headed west to Alabama. They found a wonderful home in a large tree in a new forest called the Talladega National Forest. It reminded Cameron a lot of her home in Georgia.

The family had hardly begun unpacking when they heard voices below. A large group had formed at the foot of their new tree. The new neighbors were there to welcome the Crows to their new home. "Hello there!" shouted a beaver. "Welcome! We are glad you are here." The new neighbors organized a welcome picnic so that the Crow family could meet some of their new friends.

Many animals brought special dishes to eat. Mrs. Squirrel brought a nut casserole, and Ms. Raccoon brought a corn soufflé. Even Mr. Bluejay brought an apple pie (with worms of course). Everyone ate, sang songs,

and played games. Cameron couldn't believe it when she was the first one picked for the kickball game.

By the time the sun went down, Cameron was exhausted. She had already made several new friends, and she had not even spent one night in her new home. Mom tucked Cameron in that night. "How was your day, Blossom?" she asked her. "Mom, you were right," said Cameron, "making friends is easy if you are nice to people." Cameron drifted off to sleep with dreams in her head about all the fun she would have with her new friends.

Reading Challenge

After reading "Cameron Crow," answer the following questions.

1. **Cameron was moving**
   - ○ A. from the forest to the city.
   - ○ B. from the Chattahoochee National Forest to Georgia.
   - ○ C. to live with her grandparents.
   - ○ D. from Georgia to Alabama.

2. **Why was Cameron worried?**
   - ○ A. She was scared to fly.
   - ○ B. She was shy.
   - ○ C. She didn't like the corn soufflé Ms. Raccoon made.
   - ○ D. She was afraid that she would not make new friends.

3. **Which of the following was not brought to the picnic?**
   - ○ A. corn soufflé
   - ○ B. popcorn
   - ○ C. apple pie
   - ○ D. nut casserole

4. **Place a 1, 2, 3, 4, or 5 on the line beside each sentence to put the events in the correct order.**

   _____ The Crow family lived in the Chattahoochee National Forest.

   _____ A large group gathered to welcome the Crow family.

   _____ Cameron dreamed about having fun with her new friends.

   _____ Cameron played kickball with her new friends.

   _____ Cameron was afraid no one would like her.

5. **What do you think are good qualities to have in a friend?**

   _____

   _____

   _____

   Total Correct _____

The Gift

Every year on Christmas Eve, Corinne and her family had a special tradition. They went to church, had a special dinner with family, then opened one gift. This year was not going to be the same. Dad had decided that the family should do something a little different to share the holiday spirit with families less fortunate.

Corinne was angry. She liked Christmas Eve the way it was, and she didn't want to give that up. She pouted in the back of the car as Mom and Dad told her about their plans. They were going to a place called a soup kitchen. Dad explained to Corinne that the people who came to get dinner here did not have a warm home to go home to like they did. Corinne could not believe it when her mother told her that many of the people they would be serving slept under bridges or in parks. Corinne was a little nervous.

When they got to the soup kitchen everyone was given a job to do. Mom and Dad served food to people. Corinne's job was to take bread to each table. Most of the people smiled at Corinne and thanked her. Corinne stopped at one table and stared. She was surprised to see a family holding hands with their heads bowed. The little boy looked like he could be in her second grade class.

After dinner, everyone was invited to join in some games and singing. Corinne found the courage to walk up to the little boy she had seen at dinner. "Hi, I'm Corinne," she said.

"Hi, Corinne. I'm Ronnie." Ronnie told Corinne how he and his family had been living in different shelters since his dad

got laid off from work. Corinne couldn't imagine what it must be like not to have your own room or your own bed. Ronnie told Corinne that he had a Magic Rock that someone had given him. He used it to make wishes. He used it sometimes to wish that his father would find a good job and that his family would have a home again.

Before Corinne knew it, it was time to go home. She said good-bye to Ronnie and was silent the whole ride home. Just before they got home, Corinne put her hands into her pockets. She felt something hard inside. She pulled out a round present wrapped in newspaper. She could not believe her eyes. Inside was the Magic Rock. Attached to it was a note that said:

Merry Christmas Corinne. I hope this Magic Rock works as well for you as it did for me. Tonight I wished for a friend to play with on Christmas Eve. My wish came true. Thank you for making my Christmas merry.
—Ronnie.

Corinne told her parents that she hoped that they could work at the soup kitchen every Christmas Eve. She went to bed feeling good. She hoped deep in her heart that Ronnie's family was going to be just fine. She touched the Magic Rock by her pillow. This was the best Christmas ever!

Merry Christmas Corrine From: Ronnie

Reading Challenge

After reading "The Gift," answer the following questions.

1. **What change did Corinne's family make this Christmas Eve?**
   - ○ A. They each opened one gift.
   - ○ B. They had a special dessert.
   - ○ C. They played games and sang songs.
   - ○ D. They worked in a soup kitchen.

2. **How did Corinne feel about working in the soup kitchen at the beginning of the story?**
   - ○ A. She was excited.
   - ○ B. She was angry.
   - ○ C. She was looking forward to it.
   - ○ D. She was sad.

3. **What is a soup kitchen?**
   - ○ A. a place to buy soup
   - ○ B. a fancy restaurant
   - ○ C. a place where people who don't have homes can come to eat
   - ○ D. a room in the house

4. **What did Ronnie usually use his Magic Rock to wish for?**
   - ○ A. for his dad to get a good job and for his family to find a home
   - ○ B. to make a new friend
   - ○ C. to win the game at the soup kitchen
   - ○ D. for Corinne to give him a present

5. **How did Ronnie surprise Corinne?**
   - ○ A. He sat beside her at dinner.
   - ○ B. He asked for an extra roll.
   - ○ C. He gave her his Magic Rock.
   - ○ D. He painted her a picture.

6. **Why do you think Corinne thought this was the best Christmas ever?**

   _____

7. **Do you think Corinne's family will work in the soup kitchen again? Why or why not?**

   _____

Total Correct _____

Answer Pages

Page 9, Eli
1. B 2. D 3. 4, 2, 1, 3
4. Answers will vary. He was tired.
5. Picture should show a tan, white, and brown dog.

Page 12, Arden's Surprise
1. Answers will vary. It was her birthday.
2. Answers will vary. It would ruin the surprise.
3. Underlined: milk, peanut butter, cheese, strawberries, cereal, orange juice
4. Answers will vary. She was happy that Arden remembered her birthday.
5. Baby Cate liked the unusual surprise cookie sandwich. 6. Answers will vary.
7. swim 8. bake

Page 14, Twins
1. B 2. W 3. B
4. C 5. C
6. Each picture should show some of the details described in the story.
7. Fraternal twins
8. Circle: teeth, braces, play, base, both

Page 17, The Zoo
1. A 2. C 3. B
4. D 5. C 6. D

Page 19, Pillow Fight
1. Any three of the following pairs: out-shout, inside-hide, play-say, involved-solved, room-broom, smile-pile, said-head, new-too
2. C 3. B
4. Answers will vary. They were having a sleepover.
5. Answers will vary.

Page 21, Bats
1. A 2. C 3. D
4. A myth is something people believe to be true, but is not true.
5. A bat will fly into your hair and get caught in it; and bats bite people and suck their blood.
6. Answers will vary. If caught, the bat will become scared and it may bite to get away.
7. Answers will vary. Cat, sat, pat, and fat are possible answers.

Page 24, The Summer Plan
1. D 2. B 3. C
4. 2, 1, 3, 4

Page 27, The Lonely Turtle
1. Frederick and the frog
2. B 3. D 4. A
5. Answers will vary. He was amazed and likely felt proud.
6. Yes, he painted with his new friends

Page 29, Two
1. a tree and a blade of grass
2. green
3. any two of the following: tall and small, gift and lift, spring and sing
4. She likes them. (and/or) They make her want to sing.
5. Answers will vary.

Page 32, Marvin the Moose
1. Answers will vary. There were lots of people and sailboats to watch.
2. longed
3. Yes. The paper's headline said, "Moose Wanders Bar Harbor."
4. Marvin's picture was on the front page of the paper.
5. Because humans could be dangerous.
6. Two hours
7. 2, 1, 4, 3

Page 36, Lizzy's Song
1. C 2. B 3. D
4. A
5. She sang a song.
6. Answers will vary.

Page 39, Nikki the Dog
1. 4, 3, 6, 1, 2, 5 2. C
3. C 4. B 5. A
6. C

Page 42, Lemonade
1. D 2. B 3. A
4. intersection
5. Answers may vary. It was hot. People were thirsty.
6. Answers will vary.

Page 44, The Rain
1. B 2. C 3. A
4. Pitter patter pitter pat ...
5. Answers will vary.

Answer Pages

Page 46, Insects
1. C
2. changes in the life stages of some living things
3. A   4. B   5. D

Page 48, The Pumpkin Patch
1. 5, 1, 4, 3, 2   2. D   3. B
4. C   5. A

Page 50, The Koala
1. B   2. D   3. B
4. A   5. C

Page 52, Costume Party
1. B   2. C   3. C
4. A   5. B
6. They won the first place ribbon.

Page 55, Rudy Gets Lost
1. B   2. A   3. D
4. C   5. 2, 4, 5, 3, 1

Page 57, Teddy
1. A   2. D   3. B
4. B   5. D

Page 60, Germs
1. D   2. A   3. B
4. eyes, germs, mouth, sick, sneeze;
5. Any three of the following: horsefly, raindrop, dewdrop, horseback, sawhorse, or backdrop.

Page 63, Ed and Emily
1. D   2. B   3. B
4. C   5. A
6. 3, 1, 2, 4, 6, 5

Page 66, Nana's Gift
1. C   2. B   3. C
4. D   5. A   6. 5, 3, 4, 1, 2

Page 69, Lucas
1. C   2. A   3. D
4. B   5. it's   6. doesn't
7. they'll

Page 71, Who's There?
1. B   2. C   3. D
4. A   5. D
6. Answers will vary

Page 73, Amazing Ants
1. B   2. B   3. D
4. C   5. A   6. O
7. F

Page 76, Sea Dreams
1. C   2. B   3. A
4. want   5. fish   6. watch
7. look   8. twist
9. Answers will vary.

Page 79, Americans in History
1. A   2. C   3. A
4. on the one-dollar bill   5. B

Page 82, A Little Brother
1. C   2. B   3. A
4. D   5. B

Page 86, Olivia's Dance
1. 3, 1, 5, 2, 4   2. C   3. B
4. D   5. Answers will vary.

Page 90, Cameron Crow
1. D   2. D   3. B
4. 1, 3, 5, 4, 2   5. Answers will vary.

Page 93, The Gift
1. D   2. B   3. C
4. A   5. C
6. Answers will vary.
7. Answers will vary.